MOMENT TO MOMENT

Books by Rod McKuen

POETRY:

And Autumn Came
Stanyan Street and Other Sorrows
Listen To The Warm
Lonesome Cities
Twelve Years of Christmas
In Someone's Shadow
With Love...
A Man Alone
(printed in private edition)
Fields of Wonder
Moment to Moment
Beyond the Boardwalk
The Carols of Christmas

COLLECTED LYRICS:

New Ballads
Pastorale
The Songs of Rod McKuen
Rod

Moment to Moment
ROD McKUEN

CHEVAL BOOKS

A CHEVAL BOOK
Published in the United States by Cheval Books,
8721 Sunset Blvd., Hollywood, California 90069
Library of Congress Catalog Card Number 77-188818
Manufactured in the United States of America

Designed by Hy Fujita

FIRST EDITION

This is a book for P.V.W.

**I wasn't hunting,
but I hoped.**

Portions of COMING OF AGE appeared in Woman's Own Magazine under the title *The Unfolding World of a Child*, in a slightly different form. HELEN first appeared in *If You Love Somebody Tell Them*, under the title Toward a Better Breed of Freaks. THURSDAY first appeared on the album ROD McKUEN/AMSTERDAM CONCERT.

In the main, this is a diary of a small time in
Amsterdam where little happened. But as those
times go, everything happened. There was no
future in the incident, I felt that at the time. The
only future now will belong to my memory
each time I read these poems over.

RM / 1971

Prelude: The Leaving

Lingering
as the dying do
between that life just past
and the still unknown,
I only know enough
about myself as yet
to know that I don't know enough.

Nor can I say
I know what's missing—
voids are voids
and only seen completely
after we've had victories over them.

I do not dangle
at the dawning
on a strand of sunlight,
nor do I perch on
paragraphs of prayers.
I'm hill and gully rider only
on the edge of conversations,
never in the center.

Get close enough to learn
but *lean* as little as you can
and only then
to have a closer listen.

All men have lessons
they can give you
even in rejection.
And the least
that you can offer any man
is your arm or shoulder.

There will be
times when many
will want pieces of you
but only offer up the whole.

The small times count.
The inches not the miles.
Touches not tradition
will fill your memory
in the morning or the end.

And memories are
the only sanity
the world can now assure us.

Men
while traversing
their lifetimes
should not take steps
that lead them
   year to year
or even day to decade,
only moment to moment.

So whatever interlude
of kindness or of light,
real or pretended love
you see coming
through the distance
be ready and be open.

The cost of one warm moment
is considerable
but worth the poverty
that always staying private means.

I know this and I knew it
that September night in Amsterdam.
And having been without love
for so long a time
and what new knowledge
each encounter brings
I must have been
as ready as the rose is
to be caressed
and then be ruined
    by the rain.

Moment To Moment

SATURDAY NOON

Here now the maple trees
ejaculating in the fall wind.
They'll be bare in only hours
while the wind not even breathless
will rape and rampage
on the higher hills.

Such an effortless excess,
those light limbs letting go,
but given the wind's full passion,
who would not bend to it?

The pines sweep down
the sky's broad bottom
uninterrupted by the fog
and not bedazzled by the rain.

The pines, a many-fingered broom
not pretending to be stately
or more useful
than a simple broom.

SATURDAY NIGHT

To see them dance
is quite a marvel
whether it be Strauss
    or *Stoney End.*

Their motions are as fluid
as a kind of liquid neon,
even on a floor so crowded
that each of them appears
to be the other's
next of kin.

The dancing
like the darkness
has no beginning
and no real end.

If you come here
three nights running
you begin to feel
the night starts only
with your arrival
and stops as quickly
when you go.

I wasn't dancing
but I wasn't standing still.
I wasn't hunting,
        but I hoped.
Not New Year's Eve
was in my mind,
        only now.

Then now becomes
tomorrow
with the lateness
of the hour.

Later on the street
the first fall leaves
were flying through the railings
to float along the dark canal.
Another evening maybe
but for now
the hotel bed's security
was all the sureness
I could know
and so my footsteps quickened,
for it waited in the darkness
        empty and alone.

SUNDAY NIGHT

I'm living,
no I'm *staying*,
down the street.
We can walk.

MONDAY AFTERNOON

Blinking like an owl in morning
I woke up wanting you,
For all the Denver days ahead
             and ever after.
For all the Sausalitos past
and Boston nights that ended
before they had beginnings.

Thick throated still
and not yet
             wide awake enough
I finally came alive
to find you studying me.

I wish that I
had told you then
I wasn't what you watched,
and given time to rearrange
my face and frame for you,
I'd be closer to the man
who picked you up
          the night before.

But seeing you
at my breath's edge
filled my head
with such a wonder
that I could only pray in silence
that though your eyes were open
you stared at me from sleep.

TUESDAY AFTERNOON

A cat
came off the higher roof
and down below my window,
balancing on so thin a rail
that even pigeons had not dared
that same thin rail before.

A red and yellow cat
of some age and some experience
sat the afternoon out
down below my window — waiting
as he must have known
    I waited.
A cat for company
until the sunset started
then he leisurely climbed back.

TUESDAY NIGHT

I don't know why we lie here
on the floor collecting dust
when both of us are well aware
that any bed's more comfortable
than carpet over hardwood.

Use my crooked arm as a pillow
and let my body cover you
as lightly as it can
with this bump and elbow blanket.

Now see me eye to eye. Hello.
I know why we lie here on the floor.

WEDNESDAY

I move in close,
crouching like a fighter
waiting for a chance
    an opening
a way to move in closer.

God I cannot wait much longer.
Invite me or I'll take you.
Give in quietly or go.

Are you that wild late-blooming plant?
If so you must not wait to tell me
for there's little time in this life
    and the next half's spent.

WEDNESDAY NIGHT

I don't have to touch you
to be touching you
nor feel your face
to feel your face.

Yet sometimes touching you
I feel you not at all.

THURSDAY

Bicycle bells
and barrel organs
bellowing through
the bedroom window
woke me early,
though I had been awake
an hour before,
closing my arms about you
while you barely stirred,
avoiding my face in sleep
the way new lovers always do
the first night in
the first night out.

Then sleeping again,
    at least I did,
until half opened eyes
let me observe you
dressing in that same
thick silence
that in the end
surrounded us the night before.

THURSDAY AFTERNOON

I bought red dahlias for you
and sunflowers
from across the square.
They have not yet
begun to fall.

THURSDAY EVENING

Goodbye.
I know no other way
    to say it.
What shall I call you?
    Never mind.
This poem is for you
and you will know it
in Munich or in Minnesota.

It only complicates
my life as well as yours
to get your name down here
as well as detail
inch by inch the night.

The windmills turn
and we turn too,
not with the wind
but slowly,
imperceptibly away.

Not noticed by the sunset —
        if there is one
or by anyone.
Not we ourselves.

We will not walk again
along canals together.
And the record player
will not play *We Will*.

It's somehow miracle enough
that Amstel beer in Amsterdam
made us drunk enough
to meet at all.

Still, September has a way with it
and a way of coming round
next year and the next year too.

And Thursday comes around
at least once every week.

FRIDAY

How right to love you,
across the room
across the seas
and if need be
all across a lifetime
with you or without you.

Your going is a fact,
your taking leave
with but a telephoned goodbye
almost a certainty.

I'll gain no understanding
from your absence
and any truth I fall upon
by my own hand
would have met me sooner
had you been beside me
to attract and guide it
down our double road.

SATURDAY MORNING

And now
the table's bloody
with red dahlia petals.
The sunflowers too
begin to hang their heads.

I have paced these rooms
and rolled alone
upon this bed
two dozen times today.

I've been out walking
and come back
and been out walking once again.

The street was empty
till ten-thirty.
Now it's filling up.
It seems as though
all Amsterdam
has the morning off.

My watch is running fast
or my watch is running slow.
One the other is the truth,
I'm removed from real time.

For the better part
of this one week
I've set my timepiece
by your coming
and your going.
My only clock now
.is the chiming in the square.

My sense of distance
          hasn't changed.
I still feel miles
and worlds away
from anything that was or is.

More and more
I wonder if that distance
always was and has been
as compatible as closeness.
If this is so,
that habit must be changed
or tempered by
some new truth
not yet evident
or shown to me
        for what it is.

If I'm to be a man
of dark distance set apart
from what I thought I needed,
then the distance
has to be a measured one.

THE SECOND MONDAY

Far off, nothing.
And I expect
if it were later in the day
even the horizon
would blur into
a single medium blue,
the color of cheap china.

Being near the sea has stalled
the coming of some madness
I'll meet later.
How long I keep it
at a distance
depends to some extent
upon what solace
I get from this ocean.

The truth is
no one listens.
Not to the frogs or crickets,
not to the baying of hounds
or the barking of dogs,
not even to the radio —
or the radiator's bumping.

People hear all right
but they hear only those things
they themselves have programed
and any chance of getting past
those built-in scramblers
is remote and far removed
if one can even give it that.

ANOTHER MONDAY, TWO MONTHS LATER

Now I have the time
to take you riding
    in the car
to lie with you in private deserts
or eat with you
    in public restaurants.

Now I have the time
for football all fall long
and to apologize
for little lies and big lies
told when there was no time
to explain the truth.

I am finished
with whatever tasks
kept me from walking
in the woods with you
or leaping in the Zanford sand.

I have so much time
that I can build for you
sand castles out of mortar.

Now I have the time
to see bad movies
and read bad books
    aloud to you.
I can now waste time
on you and on myself.

Mid-week picnics.
Minding my temper in traffic.
Washing your back
and cleaning out my closets.
Staying in bed with you
long past the rush hour
and the pangs of hunger.
     And listening
to the story of your life
in deadly detail
whatever time it takes,
I have that time.

I've always wanted
to watch flowers open
all the way,
however long the process took.

I'd hoped that I might
take you traveling
down the block
or to wherever,
now I have the time.

Now I have the time
to be bored
to be delivered
to be patient
to be understanding,
to give you
all the time you need.

Now I have the time.
Where are you?

Postlude: Leaving Again

1.

A phrase of love
can be strung out
in such a way
that *hate* by contrast
sounds more beautiful.

Canaries do not sing love,
and the truest lovers
cannot always say love's name
but by their actions
they speak volumes
yet unpublished and
as yet not written down.

Love stings when it should tingle
and leaves long scars
instead of deep impressions.
Worst of all
for love gone wrong
there is no warranty
or bond to cover damage.

The guarantee
for finding sanity again
is finding love again
and giving over
to the new beloved
that one facet of yourself
you held back last time.

If it should happen to you
one more time,
        and it will,
display your love
in all its Sunday clothes
for unless you go out
with your face
toward the sunlight
how are you to know?

Why is it
that in some far place,
away from home
and true or trumped up
          responsibility
we are so willing
to volunteer everything?

In ten years of traveling
giving in to love
is not exception anymore
but more the rule.

I am not alone
in letting go
and I am not unique
          in giving in.

Others take advantage
of that month
or two week span
called vacation or escape.

In truth
that time is just enough reality
to get us through
the other forty-eight
or fifty weeks.

2.

I cross the corridors
of hell these days
and pace through
     purgatory too,
and so my hour in heaven
should be assured.

Sketches Of Friends

GERALDINE

I love you as much
for what you don't
let others do to me
as I do for what
you've done for me
    yourself.

MADELINE

Hip-high in the water
Waist-high at my side
Shoulder-high together walking
you are the promise
and the prize.

Surely there will never be
enough time left
to tell you what it's like
to look up from the crowd
having worked all night
and see not just your eyes
but all of you
and all of me within them.

RALPH

Someone wrote of you
that people work a lifetime
to attain your natural innocence.
I believe that to be so,
for on seeing you
the first time out
I remember that I felt
as though I'd come upon
the living Christ.

I'm sure that when
His tongue was tangled
Christ nodded out of shyness
and that He needed other men
as you do.

You have to be a man
to care for other men.
Isn't that why God built flesh
around the spirit of His son
and made Him visible?

Jesus on a motorcycle,
hair helmetless and blowing
in the hard wind,
eyes flattened back
against His face,
riding through the northern night
safe inside the skin of Ralph.

NAN

I know our world has widened.
You went to the moon —
                    I didn't.

And so we're more apart
than just each other's houses.

I love you
as I leave these random woods.
Is it with heavy joy I leave
    or light sadness?

Whatever.
My life is broken off
and interrupted.

EDWARD

The brother I never played with
growing up a coast away.
Wintering in Fall River
and summering in Somerset
later to become the mender
of some dreams I had
that Friday friends and Sunday friends
kept battering and breaking up.

Edward,
holding me when mama died,
and never letting go.
And yet as my own brother
I own him not nor would I
but I own all the days
that he passed out and over to me
by believing in the present
however long that it might last
and giving me in ten short years
a nearly perfect past.

HELEN

Running with the pack
is not so easy
as one might suppose.
It takes a special kind of guts
to listen to the same old noise
day after day . . . even if
the peace at night's rewarding.
Going it alone has hazards too,
but you meet a better breed of freaks.

DAVID

David in the driveway leaving.
Pausing for a moment
but a moment only
there in the car
behind the wheel
and down the driveway gone.

See the night sky, David,
free of clouds at last.
Stars there are and crickets
in the trees.
All have moon blue shadows.

Pieces Of Glass

ON THE WAY TO SACRAMENTO

The three of us
on our way to Sacramento
and no one speaking.
Each having committed the error
of caring for the other —
                    but separately.

And all the while
we thought that we were different.
From what, I wonder?
Passion doesn't even need the wind,
it is a need unto itself.

Where friendship lurked
and love once lived
now only silence dwells
and truth between us
will not come again.
Though we're altogether naked
even to the autumn trees,
we are more private
than we'll ever be.

I wish that I were home
wherever that might be.
Home for always, and alone.
Not just one more
passenger of hate
on this third day of October
riding down the California highway.

I pray that I might never be
amazed and let down even once again
by those I trust.

Not possible? I know.
Then I pray
we'll all reach Sacramento soon.

YOUNG MEN

Young men
start at the top
and work their way down.

As George as any Washington
they're told they ought to be
and so they start
by chopping down
the cherry tree of life.

PIECES OF GLASS

Can the living reach the dead?
Yes, I said, as I lay dying.
And if they can't,
I heard the unknown say,
it's not from any lack of trying.

Coming Of Age

GOING ON ONE

It's never warm enough.
It's always cold.
You'd think they'd know by now
that waking me to feed me
only makes me cry again.

But then,
what's left for me?
My brain is still an embryo
that can't form sentences as yet
and I can't make a fist
quite big enough to get my way.

But wait — just wait.
Her milk of human kindness
is helping me grow stronger
    every day.

2 YEARS

They leave you alone at two
to crawl by yourself
    and
        fall
            by yourself
without much attention
and that's just to mention a few
of the things they allow
between one and three
the in-between age of two.

3 YEARS

I want to be a nurse.
And now that that's decided
I hope to be a cowboy
with my time divided
between a fireman and teacher.
I haven't any black clothes yet,
so I couldn't be a preacher.

5 YEARS

Where did I come from?
                    Why me?

Who carried me up
over the sunrise
into the time of day?
Away from whatever
I don't remember.

With Daddy away at work
and Mother making bread
how did I make it up the hill?
(We live on a hill, you know
you go slow to get there
and slow going down
and this is my house,
but how did I find it?
I must have had help
the first time around.
I don't think this house
is on anyone's map
for it belongs to me and my
    mother.
And Daddy, of course.)

7 YEARS

Now that I'm seven
reaching for ten
I don't think I'll ever be
    six again.

9 YEARS

I must mow the lawn come Saturday.
Thank God I'm not quite tall enough
to trim the backyard trees.

Woodcutting will come next, I'm sure,
and mending fences too.
Even now they let them rot
in preparation, I suppose
for those birthdays in the distance.

We'll play football on another day
unless the family buys a goat
before the weekend's out.

10 YEARS

I'm learning to drink tea
and how to say "yes please"
and "no thank you, not today".
The knife is on the right side
      of the setting,
where I supposed the fork should be.
Good morning and good evening
       and good day,
A time to live, a time to die,
but not much time to play.

13 YEARS

Today she smiled at me,
A queer sort of look
of a crooked smile
that made me all red,
    outside and in.

I didn't much like it
but I didn't half wish
tomorrow she'd do it again.

14 YEARS

Of course I smoke.
Do you find that surprising?
Men of my age have always smoked
and chewed if that was their pleasure.

Yes I find the world a mess.
If I were Prime Minister
    I'd change all that.
There'd be freedom for wenching
and belching in school
no caning for bunking
or strutting about
and teachers who differed
would be sorted out.

15 YEARS

They are at it again.
She says I'm spoiled.
He says I'm not.
(Of course she's right,
but I find as I grow older
it's best I don't choose sides.)

17 YEARS

I am wounded —
and I won't be well again.
Not the tape of triumph
or the bandage of bright victory
could mend for me this wound
she's given by the act of leaving.

Had she left the room,
had she gone forever
or across the street,
gone is gone
and it would be the same.

I die daily now
and we didn't even call it love.

18 YEARS

I've been waiting all this time
thinking that the world was waiting
just beyond my world for me.

What did I expect to find?
Something more than what I see
upon my parents' tired faces.
Something more than what
they fill their lives with
even if that something's only me.

World, you'd better have
that something ready
or I'll make it for my own.

About The Author

ROD McKUEN was born in Oakland, California, and
has traveled extensively throughout the world both as
a concert artist and a writer. In less than five years his
books of poetry have sold over seven million copies in
hard cover, making him the best selling and most widely
read poet of all times. In addition he is the best selling
living author writing in any hard cover medium today.
Though his books do not appear in soft back, his songs
and poetry have been translated into Spanish, French,
Dutch, German, Russian, Czechoslovakian, Japanese,
Chinese, Norwegian and a dozen other languages.
His film music has twice been nominated for Motion
Picture Academy Awards. His songs have sold over 100
million records and his classical music, including his
1st & 2nd symphonies and his concertos for guitar and
harpsichord are performed by leading orchestras
throughout Europe. Cleveland Amory has written in
Saturday Review, "Rod McKuen is the country's No. 1
one-man communications empire."
Despite what appears to be an extremely heavy work
load, the author spends a good deal of time at home in
California in a rambling Spanish house with a menagerie
of Old English Sheep Dogs and 5 cats. He likes
outdoor sports and driving. His latest book of poetry
AND TO EACH SEASON will be co-published by
Cheval Books and Simon & Schuster in the fall of 1972.